you & your wedding

The BEST MAN'S Book

you & your wedding®

The BEST MAN'S Book

Maia Morris

foulsham
LONDON • NEW YORK • TORONTO • SYDNEY

foulsham

The Publishing House, Bennetts Close, Cippenham, Slough,
Berkshire, SL1 5AP, England

Foulsham books can be found in all good bookshops and direct from
www.foulsham.com

ISBN: 978-0-572-03366-8

A CIP record for this book is available from the British Library

Printed in Dubai

Contents

Introduction

Don't panic! The best man's job may seem a bit daunting – and if it doesn't you obviously haven't fully realised what it involves yet – but with a bit of guidance and a few helpful survival tips you'll come through it all right. Now get reading…

Congratulations! First and foremost, being asked to be someone's best man is a huge compliment. Whatever you may think about the task before you, someone has chosen you out of all his close friends and family as the person most able to see him through the best day of his life and the run-up to it. It will be you he turns to for advice before the big day and it will be you he calls for a swift beer when his bride-to-be starts to display dangerously volatile 'bridezilla' symptoms (if you don't know the signs, take a look at page 69!). Most importantly, he will put his general well-being in your hands when it comes to the stag night.

Why you?

You'll probably know the answer to this already, but undoubtedly you've been chosen because you are one of the groom's best friends, his brother or even his dad – or maybe you've been through a lot with him in the past. You may think that perhaps you're not the right man for the job, that the groom may have other friends who are much better at organising a party or are far more adept at public speaking, but he's chosen you regardless of whether that's the case because you're the person he would most like to do it – and he's sure you'll make a good job of it.

Where to start?

You may have just heard the news, accepted gladly and then rushed out to buy this book to make sure you're immediately up to speed on what you need to do. However,

a more likely scenario is: the wedding has been steadily drawing nearer for few months and some kind/concerned female – either the bride or your girlfriend – has plonked this book on your lap as a subtle hint that you really should be getting a move on. Whichever is the case, you're reading the book now and that's all that matters.

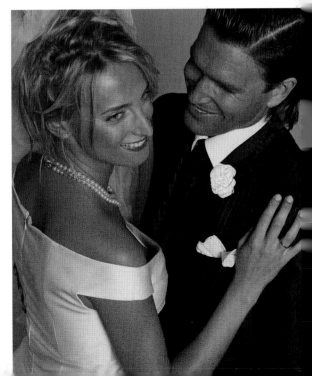

As grooms editor of *You & Your Wedding* magazine, and having organised my own wedding, I've had plenty of experience in advising the men in the wedding party on how best to get through the big day, and I've included chapters on all the major responsibilities that fall to the best man. You're probably well aware that the stag night and a speech are on your must-do list in big, bold print – and I've allocated plenty of space to both these tasks – but there are lots of other less well advertised jobs with your name against them too. Things such as finding cool transport, organising all the other men in the wedding party and looking after the buttonholes and the orders of service are just a few obvious ones, but a really good best man will also throw himself into the job in hand by dancing with elderly aunties at the reception, sorting out the newlyweds' luggage and being able to cope with any kind of disaster that may crop up before the bride and groom are even aware it's happened.

With the huge numbers of books, magazines and websites out there today advising brides-to-be on exactly what they should expect from everyone, you're right to feel a little nervous. You wouldn't want to come between a frenzied bride and her perfect dream of wedding happiness now, would you? Not only will this book prove to be an essential guide, it could well be your saving grace in the minefield of potential faux pas that is the modern day wedding.

Rise to the challenge

The real trouble with being asked to be a best man is that, no matter how flattered you are and how much you realise it's an honour to be asked, it's a difficult job that lots of guys would rather not have to do. If you really truly feel that you aren't up to it, then it's perfectly acceptable to turn down the offer – just make sure you think long and hard before you do. You may well regret it and, more importantly, once you've read through this book you'll see that there's nothing – well almost nothing – to it. Trust me, as long as you're well prepared and put in the work, you'd be hard pressed to make a complete hash of it. And if you've just bought this book and there are only three weeks to go until the wedding, then even though you're going to have to read a bit faster and work a bit harder it's still possible to do a great job.

Finally, apologies to any female best 'men' who may be leafing though this book and having to put up with the constant use of the male pronoun – I've made the assumption that 99 per cent of those reading will be male. None of the advice is particularly gender-specific, so hopefully you'll find it all just as helpful as the next 'man'.

So without further ado, let's get this show on the road…

What's Expected of You?

There are one or two expectations

riding on the best man at any wedding, with everyone
from the guests to the vicar wanting a piece of you.
The best – and only – solution is to be prepared.

Everyone who attends a wedding has some expectation of the best man, no matter how small. The guests will expect you to know where to go after the wedding breakfast or where the cloakroom at the reception is, and the bride's expectations can run to pages and pages – half of which she'll probably expect you to know as if by magic. The way to meet her expectations is planning. To start, here's an outline of the traditional best man's duties.

SURVIVAL TIP 1

Before you do anything else, check the wedding date in your diary. There's no point in reading any further if there's something on that day you simply can't get out of. Assuming it's free, then also block out all the evenings of the preceding week, and if possible take one or two days off just before the wedding, and definitely the day after for essential recovery time.

Before the wedding

- Organise a stag night.
- Help the groom choose the ushers.
- Help choose outfits for the male members of the wedding party and co-ordinate everyone for fittings.
- Help choose the wedding day transport.
- Write the best man's speech.
- Attend the rehearsal.
- Look after the groom the night before the wedding.

On the day

- Get the groom to the church on time, with the wedding rings.
- Co-ordinate the ushers, making sure they all have their outfits and cufflinks etc and know where they're supposed to be when.
- Hand out orders of service with the ushers and show guests where to sit.
- Calm the groom's nerves before the ceremony.
- Make sure all the guests have transport between the ceremony and the reception.
- Help organise the wedding party and guests for the formal photographs.
- Make sure that any wedding gifts are put somewhere safe.
- Act as toastmaster (if there isn't one) for the other speechmakers.
- Give out thank you gifts during the speeches.
- Make a great speech.
- Take charge of paying the celebrant (that's the vicar, priest or registrar to you and me) and also the band.
- Take to the dance floor with the chief bridesmaid after the first dance.
- Generally help out wherever needed, acting the host, making small talk with lonely guests and checking that the bride and groom have everything they need.
- Liaise with venue staff over any problems.
- Help to tidy up at the end of the day if necessary, collecting up decorations, wedding presents, flowers, cameras etc.
- Return hire suits the day after the wedding.

The perfect best man is someone who's organised and fun and more than happy to turn their hand to anything that needs doing. You also have to stay sober enough on the stag night to ensure that the groom has a good time and gets home in one piece and to be able to give your speech on the big day. You'll need to put your all into being helpful on the day of the wedding, including everything from stepping in to help the videographer if his assistant doesn't turn up to taking Auntie Mavis for a spin on the dance floor when 'Lady in Red' comes on. And when the lights go on at the end of the night you have to help tidy up too. It's not all glamour, unfortunately.

What's Expected of You

The groom

This is where your main responsibilities lie, with the good friend who got you into this mess in the first place. When he first asked if you'd do him the honour, hopefully your first thoughts were happy ones. No doubt he will have been expecting you to be chuffed to bits to have been asked. Ideally you will have taken the news well and accepted – maybe safe to assume seeing as you've got as far as reading this book. The following is your job description from the groom's point of view.

- He will expect you to arrange a stag do for him and all his good mates, get him fairly drunk and possibly get him a stripper. More on that in Chapter 3.
- He will also expect you to be his right hand man in the run-up to the wedding, providing advice and practical help.
- He may want your help in finding outfits for all the men in the wedding party, as well as in co-ordinating everyone so that they are in the same place at the same time for fittings etc.
- Finding wedding transport may also fall into your remit.
- If the groom is particularly disorganised, he may expect you to help him with any number of his own responsibilities on top of your own.
- He may also need a little moral support if his bride and/or family are putting undue wedding pressure on him.
- He'll be expecting you to give the best man's speech after the ceremony.
- And finally, he'll generally be expecting you to take the pressure off him throughout the wedding day when it comes to organising people and solving potential problems so he can relax and enjoy himself.

SURVIVAL TIP 2

Get in there early and prove to the bride that she has nothing to worry about. Arrange a meeting with both the bride and the groom to get the lay of the land. Take this book with you to help assure her that you're on the case with all the organising, speech writing etc and she has nothing to worry about – even if it's a little bit of a white lie. And never forget that while your loyalty is with the groom, the bride is ultimately all powerful. Don't contradict anything she says about the wedding day or you may not live to see another one!

If you're still having serious concerns about whether you actually want the job, now is the time to voice them. Have a chat with the groom and tell him which areas you're worried about and try to find out what exactly he expects from you. He should know you well enough to realise what you are and aren't good at, and if he doesn't then why are you his best man?!

If you're terrified of making the speech or you think that your organisational skills aren't really up to the job, it's probably already crossed his mind. He may be able to reassure you that he knows your speechmaking skills aren't as great as Bob's, for example, but he wants you to do it and is entirely happy if you keep the speech short and sincere. He may only be expecting a night down the local for his stag night, in which case your poor organisational skills may not have to be tested. Whatever it is, chat to him first and put your mind at rest.

The bride

Now here's the tricky part. Different brides will have hugely varying expectations of how much the best man should do. There are those who will present the best man with a minute-by-minute schedule of the day and the best man's role in it, whereas others will take a more relaxed attitude, simply expecting you to turn up, give a speech and get a bit drunk.

Essentially, what the bride wants from you is to help ensure that the day runs smoothly and nothing untoward occurs to spoil her perfect wedding day. On top of the main responsibilities listed above, most brides will also expect you to do the following jobs:

- Bring the groom back from the stag night unharmed and ideally unblemished – well, at least in all the places that will show up in the photos.
- Help the groom complete his own pre-wedding jobs such as outfits and transport satisfactorily.
- Avoid getting the groom drunk the night before the wedding.
- Keep all the ushers under control and ensure they turn up wearing the right outfits and with clean hair.
- Get the groom to the ceremony well ahead of time.
- Guard the rings with your life.
- Give a speech that, while amusing, doesn't embarrass her too much or shock any of her elderly relatives.

Bridesmaids

The chief bridesmaid is potentially your main ally in this whole situation and can definitely act as your wing man on the big day, helping to sort out any problems and warning you if you're about to do/doing something that the bride doesn't like. The wedding cliché is that, caught up in the romance of the day, the best man and one

of the bridesmaids will end up having a little tête-à-tête. Don't go there; it could potentially cause a whole heap of problems and mean that everyone will forget all your good work and hilarious speech and simply remember you for snogging one of the bridesmaids.

Mother of the bride

Start off on the right foot with the mother of the bride and she'll love you forever. Make sure she's happy throughout the reception. Don't regale the guests with stories about the

groom that will make her wish she'd never let her daughter sign the register, and take her out on the dance floor before the night is over. Not only will you make your life easier but the groom will thank you for it too. Apply all these rules to the mother of the groom as well, just to be on the safe side.

Guests

For the guests, you and the other ushers will be the first port of call if they have any questions. They may not know anyone else at the wedding, and your outfit marks you out as someone who should know what's what. Even if they know almost everyone else, there's no guarantee that anyone will know the general plan for the day – unlike you. Be prepared to be Mr Helpful all day long, pointing guests in the right direction for the ceremony, the photographs, the meal, the taxi rank, even the toilets. If you spot anyone looking a bit lost, it's your job to approach them and offer your assistance. This also goes for the venue staff, because there's no guarantee they'll know where the flowers are supposed to be or who to tell about a problem with the catering – exactly the kind of queries the bride and groom shouldn't end up having to deal with on what is supposed to be the best day of their lives.

Just the two of us

What if you're not alone? Quite often grooms find it completely impossible to choose just one best man and end up choosing two or even three of their close friends. There are two ways you can look at this: you might feel a little miffed that you haven't been singled out as the one and only true best man OR you can count your lucky stars that you'll be able to split all the jobs in this book between both or all of you, not to mention that you won't have to stand up and do the speech on your own. You can divide up the roles equally, such as one of you taking responsibility for organising the stag night transport while the other finds a venue, and then when it comes to the speech either do it as a double act or each stand up separately and give shorter individual speeches that complement each other. If you know the groom from school, for example, you could cover his early years, while the other best man could talk about his later life.

What should *you* expect from the modern wedding?

These days lots of couples just aren't satisfied with the local church hall, a few sausages on sticks and the DJ they went to school with. The modern wedding can be anything from 20 guests in a restaurant to an extravaganza of flowers and cake, with hundreds of guests. This all takes a mammoth amount of planning, and therefore stress, and you as best man are an integral part of this process.

This doesn't mean that you can't have a fantastic time in the bargain. Whatever the size of the wedding, once your speech is done you're mostly off duty. As well as carrying out the odd helpful task, you'll also be able to participate in the eating, drinking, dancing and general carousing that will be going on. And if you get yourself organised ahead of time, there's no reason why you shouldn't be able to fulfil all your duties and join in with the partying. Read on to find out where to start.

First Things First

Most weddings are planned six months to a year in advance,
but it isn't unusual for a couple to decide to get married next
month or, on the other hand, in two or three years' time. Although
it's a fair bet that those of you who had three years' advance
warning only bought this book six months before the wedding
– at most – didn't you?

Choosing the ushers

The groom may well ask for your advice on choosing the ushers. Generally they will be other close friends, brothers or future brothers-in-law. You'll probably know one or all of them. The ushers will act as your back-up in organising the stag night and on the big day, and hopefully you'll be able delegate a few jobs to them. If you don't know all of them well, you could ask the groom to arrange a night out together so you can get to know one another and swap stag night ideas. Make sure you get all their contact details such as mobile numbers and email addresses to save yourself the trouble later.

There may also be some ushers in their teens or younger who are relatives of the bride or groom. It will probably be your job to look after them on the day and check they're not causing any trouble. Hopefully they will look up to you as a paragon of knowledge and experience and this won't be a problem, but if they're a bit more of a handful and don't seem to be paying any attention to your words of wisdom, consider having some handy bribing tools with you – chocolate, card games or the promise of a (small!) sip of your beer later should do the trick.

SURVIVAL TIP 3

If you use the 'I'm just going out with the groom to talk wedding plans' excuse for going to the pub more than once a month it will cease to be believable – no matter how hands-on the groom is and how good a best man you are.

There may also be even younger pageboys in the wedding party, but generally it will fall to their parents or to the bridesmaids rather than you to manage them. If you are unlucky enough to be asked to take charge of two screaming five-year-olds on top of everything else, this is one of those jobs that you can immediately delegate to one of the other ushers – you're in charge, take advantage of it.

The engagement party

This is your first chance to shine in the role of Best Man Extraordinaire and show everyone what you're made of. This may well also be the first time you meet some of the bride's and groom's family. Make sure you turn up on time and smartly dressed, and definitely don't drink too much. If you can't behave yourself at the engagement party, you can forgive family members for worrying about what you might get up to at the reception.

Make a point of introducing yourself to the people you don't know, particularly the parents of the happy couple. It's worth making a mental note of some of the family dynamics too – such as who gets on with whom, who would be helpful in a crisis, and who's best left sitting at the bar. Most importantly, do the mothers of the bride and groom get on? You don't want to be stuck in the middle!

The final person you should really give some thought to is the father of the bride. There's a good chance he may be sinking a lot of his hard-earned cash into this wedding and he won't want you to mess the whole thing up by making a totally inappropriate speech or getting plastered and being sick in the venue's fountain. You are also a representative of the groom and if he has any concerns about the man his daughter is marrying he doesn't need to have them confirmed by finding out that the groom's best friend is a useless oaf. Seek him out at the engagement party, buy him a beer and have a long man-to-man chat about something you know he likes, such as football, golf or fly fishing – do your research first!

Money, money, money

The only other thing to consider at the moment is finances. It's not only the bride and groom and their parents who are often expected to spend money like it's going out of fashion at a modern-day wedding. A recent survey found that the average best man can spend somewhere in the region of £500, what with the cost of the stag night, a hotel for the wedding night, the wedding present and probably plenty of rounds of drinks at the bar.

Hopefully, by getting organised early on you'll be able to avoid some of the costs that fall to the disorganised best man who doesn't collect stag night money early enough and has to cover the shortfall himself or ends up forking out for taxis because he hasn't planned ahead and arranged transport. All the same, if you're not made of money, it might be worth putting a little bit aside each month so that by the time of the wedding you have a some spare cash saved up.

3

The Stag Night

Forget arranging the transport and escorting the bridesmaids, apart from the speech this is what your job is really all about, giving your mate a great send-off.

Stag nights loom large in every man's life as something they've heard stories about from a very young age. There are the urban myths of grooms left naked in the street chained to a lamppost or put on the Edinburgh sleeper sozzled and wearing only their underpants the night before the wedding. There are also those hapless fellows who foolishly let their mates remove their eyebrows with a blunt razor and have to draw them back in for the wedding photos.

You've probably been on stag nights, or have friends who have, and know that, as a rule, that kind of thing doesn't happen very often. Most guys on a stag night actually really like the groom – which is why he asked them on the stag night in the first place! And while they're happy to embarrass him, get him drunk and generally take the mickey out of him all night, they don't really want to:

- make him miss his own wedding
- make him look like a complete loser on the big day because half his body hair has gone missing
- feel the wrath of his irate bride.

Let's get started...

So assuming that you do actually want to give the groom a good night rather than one that will cause him permanent injury, the best course of action is to find out what he would really like to do. Ideally, the stag night should be three or four weeks before

the wedding – any nearer and there's the possibility he might still be feeling the effects on the day. Start planning about six months before the wedding, although if you're feeling organised even earlier can't hurt. Arrange to meet up with the groom to discuss the stag night and try and get an idea from him about each of the following:

- a rough idea of numbers.
- how much he would like it to cost.
- when he would like to do it.
- whether he wants to go abroad or stay closer to home.
- whether he wants a whole weekend or just a night.
- whether he wants to do any activities, and if so whether he has any in mind.
- what he might like to do in the evening.
- anything he absolutely does not want to do.

Joint stag and hen nights

The groom may decide that he wants to have a joint stag and hen night with his fiancée. If that's the case, you'll need to speak to the chief bridesmaid and start arranging things with her. If it is going to be a joint affair, you might want to plan for something a little more sedate – and cancel any plans you had for strippers, lap dancers and so on (unless the chief bridesmaid says that as long as there are male strippers too, the bride would be happy!). Organising a rented cottage for the weekend is a good idea, as it means that in the daytime the stags and hens can head off and do their own activities and then get back together in the evening for dinner and drinks.

Whether it's a joint stag and hen night or a lads-only one, the two things you need to decide on by the end of your discussions with the groom at this point are a definite date and a list of all the people he would like to invite, along with their phone numbers and email addresses so you can start contacting them all.

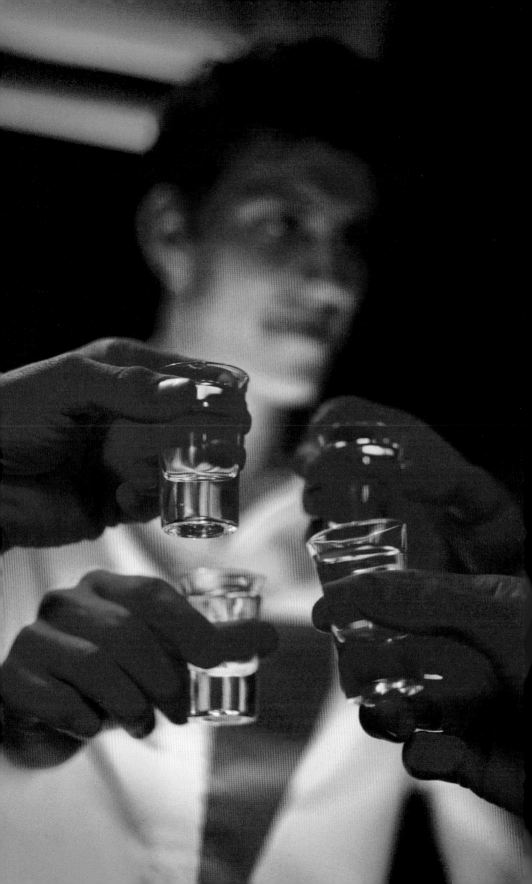

Who to invite?

This is obviously up to the groom, but organising a stag night with 20 or more people can be a bit tricky and the event may end up totally out of control. If the list seems very long, remind the groom that he's not expected to invite everyone he knows, only those people he has a long-standing and close relationship with. There's no need to include every distant cousin or work colleagues he doesn't see out of work. The only people he really should invite even if he doesn't know them well are the bride's brothers, as this is a great chance to get to know any future brothers-in-law before the wedding.

Meet the parents

There is a chance that the groom may want to – or feel that he has to – invite his father and possibly the father of the bride. Although this isn't expected, if he gets on exceptionally well with either, then there's no reason why he shouldn't invite them. Before asking either of them, make sure he's fully considered whether it's really a good idea for his prospective father-in-law to see him on a big night out with the lads before

his daughter signs on the dotted line. Of course, it all depends what kind of stag night you're planning. If you know the evening is going to be a bit raucous, you could suggest inviting his father and the father of the bride to just the daytime activities rather than the whole event.

The next step...

Before you email everyone and find out when they're free, you need to have a rough idea of where you're going and what you're going do. There's no point emailing 20 people with just the date because they'll all email you straight back with questions about what it's going to cost, how many nights it's going to be and whether it'll be near where they live so they don't have to drive too far. You might as well wait until you have more of a plan worked out.

Where?

Hopefully the groom will have given you some idea of whether he wants the stag night in the next street, the next town or the next country. These days, stag nights can range from a simple night down the local pub to a long weekend in Las Vegas with all the trimmings.

Going abroad

Great overseas destinations include:

- Amsterdam
- Barcelona
- Budapest
- Dublin
- Ibiza
- Prague
- Tallin.

There are lots of great companies (see page 116 for contacts) offering fantastic overseas packages that include accommodation, activities, dinner and entertainment, and often someone to show you round and guide you in the right direction – handy in a foreign country, especially if none of you speak the language.

Going abroad: the pros

- Don't underestimate how being in a foreign country and taking people out of their normal stamping ground can encourage a group of lads to bond, particularly if none of you have been there before.
- You'll get to sample all of the delights of a foreign city, potentially art, culture and fine cheeses, but more likely cheap booze, alluring foreign ladies and possibly firing AK47s – which you can do, for example, in Estonia.

Going abroad: the cons

- It's more likely to mean a whole weekend rather than a single night away and so will almost certainly be more expensive – not to mention the cost of the flights. This is likely to mean that some of your mates just won't be able to come. If you go all out and pick the Las Vegas option, unless all your friends are in a rather exulted wage bracket the chances are that only a small number will be able to make the trip.
- You may have to consider your friends' work and family commitments. If a lot of them are teachers, for example, they may find it hard to get a Friday off to fly to Prague, whereas if most of them are students it will probably be a lot easier.

- If you do run into any problems, which is quite possible on a stag do – particularly if you factor in locals who are a tad unhappy that their pretty town has become the number one stag destination for 2007 – being hundreds of miles from home and not speaking the language can be a big disadvantage.

Staying in the UK

If heading abroad sounds too expensive or just too much trouble, never fear because the UK is packed with great stag night destinations. Popular ones include:

- Blackpool
- Birmingham
- Brighton
- Edinburgh
- Liverpool

- London
- Manchester
- Newcastle
- Newquay
- Nottingham.

Transport

Before picking your favourite city, think about where most of the stags are based, how you would travel there and if you want to stay one night or two. You should consider whether you want to take the train or drive, and therefore how many cars you would need to take everyone. Alternatively, you could hire a minibus for the whole trip. The only problem with driving individual cars or a minibus is obviously the morning after – drinking and driving is certainly not a good way to end a great weekend, and if you've had a lot the night before you may not be safe to drive for some time the following day. Individual cars at least mean that none of you has to start the journey home before you feel ready to, but with a minibus the designated driver may feel pressurised to leave before he's happy to drive or, more sensibly, may have to curtail his drinking the night before. You could ask around and see if anyone has a friend of a friend who would be willing to act as driver if you cover his accommodation and food and also offer him a few extra quid. If there are 10 or 15 of you, this could work out a fair bit cheaper than getting a number of cabs, and it's a better option than risking not being sober enough to drive the next day.

SURVIVAL TIP 4

You can often arrange very cheap train travel if you book well in advance. It's generally a case of finding out from the train companies when the tickets go on sale and getting on the phone straight away, as there's normally a limited number of cheap ones for each train journey.

Accommodation

If you're planning to make a night or a whole weekend of it, you'll need some kind of accommodation. If you're not too far from home you may be able to use the groom's house or your own as somewhere to crash. Other good options include budget hotels, which these days offer some great deals. If you book far enough in advance some chains offer rooms for as little as £10 a night, but this will require some forward planning. If your tastes tend towards something a bit more luxurious that's great, but do bear in mind that as a general rule the posher the hotel the better behaved they will expect you to be (although any hotel can ask you to leave if you're disturbing other guests). Try not to advertise the fact that you're on a stag night if at all possible and remember that you may well be held responsible for the other guys' behaviour if you are the one who has made the booking.

Activities

Stags these days have never had it so good with the amount of jaw-droppingly exciting activities available to them. You, on the other hand, have the tricky job of finding one that suits everybody's budget and accommodates their phobias, while at the same time proving to be ten times more exciting than your other mate's do where everyone went sky diving or that bloke in accounts' who took his stags to the North Pole.

Classic stag activities that most people will enjoy include paintballing, go-karting, quad biking, white-water rafting, golf, five-a-side football, windsurfing and 4x4 driving. If you're after some more unusual options, consider the following ideas:

- Tank-driving: some companies even offer tanks that fire paintballs – ingenious!
- Flying a MIG jet: hugely expensive, so perhaps one just for the groom, but can you imagine the rush?!
- Hovercraft racing: racing around like demons while hovering above the ground as if by magic.
- Zorbing: you're strapped into a giant inflatable ball and then rolled down a hill, praying you're not going to be sick.
- Medieval jousting: if you've always had a hankering for chainmail, this is the stag activity for you.
- Human table football: like normal five-a-side but strapped to a long pole, so at least you won't have to run quite as far.
- Stuntman training: learn how to fall down a flight of stairs and leap out of open windows without killing yourself.
- A male spa: no this isn't dodgy – if you and your friends are a little too suave and sophisticated for paintballing, why not start the afternoon at a male-friendly spa where you can enjoy a proper shave or a massage while drinking beers and watching sports on TV?

- An organised tour of a whisky distillery or a visit to Vinopolis in London: try a few tasty wines – great for drinks connoisseurs.
- Horse racing: head to the races, get dressed up, place a few bets and then spend all your winnings at the bar – brilliant!
- Golf: why not head to St Andrews in Scotland for a long weekend and combine a couple of rounds with a tour of a distillery and a night on the town?

SURVIVAL TIP 6

It's always best if you can organise everything yourself – it gives it that personal touch – but if you're short on time or ideas, you could consider letting a pro take over. There are lots of great companies (see page 116) who will take almost all the work off your hands and put together a package of activities. You'll probably end up paying more for their services but shared between a big group of stags the cost shouldn't work out at too much extra per person.

Bear in mind that a lot of stag night activity organisers are very hot on spotting groups who have been drinking before taking part, or even drinking heavily the previous night, and can make you take a breath test if they think you're over the limit. This isn't the case only for driving sports and extreme activities but also for seemingly safer options such as five-a-side football, where you could potentially injure other people if you are over the limit. Make sure everyone knows this, as one person could get your whole group barred.

Sporting events

If the groom loves football or sport in general, think about combining his stag night with a major sporting event. Going to watch some rugby, football or cricket, for example, makes for a great day out with your mates. Some stag night companies offer trips such as heading to Madrid for an afternoon to watch Real Madrid play, before a night on the town sampling the local tapas and vino.

Making it economical

There are enough activities out there to suit most budgets, but it's always a good idea to give everyone a choice about what they will participate in. If some of the stags just can't stretch to the cost of the go-karting, for example, arrange to meet up with them afterwards so they can still join you for the evening. If everyone would rather save their money for a night out on the town, with a little imagination you can arrange plenty of activities that will cost you next to nothing. You could try these ideas:

- Arrange to meet in the local park and organise a classic 'jumpers for goalposts' football match before you head out for the evening.
- Reserve a space in your local pub and organise a quiz for the stag group, including plenty of embarrassing questions about the groom, some good forfeits, a couple of prizes for the winners and a booby prize for the loser – who will obviously be the groom!
- Organise an afternoon of poker.
- Have a pool competition.
- Organise a pub crawl, but pick pubs that also have interesting games such as darts, bar billiards and jenga, and have a different challenge in each one.
- Arrange a treasure hunt, taking in a few of the local pubs on the way.

Remember to be realistic about how much you can cram into one day and allow time for heading back to home-base to spruce up before going out in the evening. Remember that organising a group of people will always take much longer than you expect.

Evening activities

Here are a few ideas you might like to think about:

- A night at the dogs: you can't beat greyhound racing for combining sport, beer and betting in one fell swoop.
- A party bus: lots of stag night companies offer a party bus service, where you are ferried around town with plenty of drinks and given VIP entry into a number of different clubs.
- A casino: and if that's a bit too pricey, set up some gambling games at home and play for small change.

- Comedy clubs: generally a great night out, and you can often combine food and drinks with entertainment, as well as a club atmosphere after the comedy acts have finished.
- A strip or lap dancing club: the stag classic – in a few weeks your mate is going to promise never to look at another woman again, so this is the least you can do for him!
- A party boat: enjoy a few drinks while cruising up and down the river – not suitable for any grooms who can't swim (just in case!).
- A party fire engine: yes, it's true – www.thestagcompany.com offers an evening out in a converted fire engine, complete with a fully stocked bar (and all the stags get their own fireman outfit!).

Covering the whole gamut of available stag night activities would take up the rest of this chapter and probably the book, so turn to page 116 for a full list of stag night companies and the myriad options on offer, from a quiet night at the theatre right through to bacchanalian orgies.

Whatever you do, don't count on just heading out for a night on the town and making it up as you go along – it won't work. You'll end up in some dodgy old boozer drinking warm beer with old men. Find out which pubs and clubs are stag night-friendly before you plan your route. Write all your information down and take it out with you – you could even make copies for the stags in case you lose any of them along the way. Obviously there will be a few jibes about what an organised geeky saddo you are, but take it on the chin – it will only be coming from the guys who couldn't organise the proverbial piss-up in a brewery.

Getting sorted

Once you have a rough idea of where you want to go, how you want to get there and what kind of activities you want to indulge in, you can run your general plan past the groom – leaving out any surprises obviously. Once he's give the okay, you can start contacting the stags. Don't include the groom in your email, as he shouldn't be involved in how Bill's going to get down from Scotland or whether his cousin has the cash for the full weekend. He'll have enough on his plate as it is.

In your email include the following:

- the proposed date
- the destination
- accommodation and travel plans, with costs
- proposed daytime and evening activities
- a rough idea of the total cost – no one will mind if this changes slightly before being finalised, but people will need an estimate of what they can expect to spend
- the deadline by which you need everyone to reply – be strict with this as it's easy for people to forget, which will delay you booking activities etc and possibly cause you to miss out
- who you are and your contact details.

If anyone doesn't get back to you by the deadline give them a call and remind them. If they still haven't responded a week later, you're allowed to strike them off the list.

Cash flow

Once you have definite numbers you can get going and book your activities, transport and any accommodation. This is the point where you will have to start asking for money from people – never an easy task.

It's a good idea to have a separate bank account for all the stag night cash so you know exactly what you've got and if there's anything left at the end. In theory, if you're really organised, you could suggest to people that six months before the stag night they start paying into the account monthly so that by the time it arrives there's a nice wad of cash and no one has really felt the pinch. Unfortunately, in reality it's hard to get everyone this organised.

It's most likely that you will need to ask people for a lump sum a couple of months before the stag night. You may also want to add a bit extra onto the basic amount to cover things such as meals out, T-shirts, games and so on. Let everyone know exactly what the money will be covering and also tell them if there are any aspects of the stag night, such as night club entry or breakfast the next day, that won't come out of the joint fund. That way everyone can budget for the event.

SURVIVAL TIP 7

Insist on getting payment up front so you don't end up footing the bill, and include your bank details when you send out the email about money. That way some money can be paid straight into your account and you won't have to deal with 15 cheques and a lot of odd bits of cash.

Paying for the groom?

It's the norm for all the groom's costs to be covered by the rest of the stags, so don't forget to factor them in when you're working out what each person should pay. The general exceptions to this rule are flights if you're going abroad, and hugely lavish events, such as for example a stag do in Las Vegas, which you couldn't expect his mates to cover.

Once bookings have been confirmed and paid for, you're well on your way and, hopefully, still have a month or two to arrange some other top stuff. Extra touches such as a beer kitty, games and a few jokes to play on the stag are what turn an okay stag night into a really good one. You'll be putting the effort in for the groom's sake

of course, but don't forget that you'll also reap the benefits by having a brilliant time yourself. Those who attend will think of you forever after as 'a really great guy' – and hopefully buy you lots of drinks at the wedding!

Stag night themes, pranks and games

If you want to make sure that the stag night doesn't end up like your normal Saturday night on the town, give it a theme. There's nothing that gets stags bonding quite like being in the middle of town wearing nothing but togas, i.e. everyone's old bed sheets. Good ideas include:

- Cowboys: jeans and a checked shirt with classic cowboy hat – an added bonus is that you can also have water pistols.
- Grecian toga party: the aforementioned bed sheets – but not ideal for a winter stag night.
- James Bond: brilliant because your outfit should pass muster for even the strictest night club dress code.
- Golf bores: everyone gets out their favourite diamond-patterned jumper and best 'smart casual' pressed slacks.
- Old ladies: head to the charity shop for some comedy old lady dresses, saving the 'best' one for the groom.

If full-on costumes are a bit too much, you can go for matching T-shirts instead. You know the type – 'Johnny's Stag Tour 2007' for example. Or be a bit more inventive and add pictures of the groom, or theme the T-shirts along the lines of his favourite film or football team.

SURVIVAL TIP 8

Costumes may not make your life easier if you're trying to get into restaurants or night clubs. If possible, check with prospective venues as well as any activity centres about dress codes – you don't want your Superman cape to get caught in the wheel of your go-kart! Or just wear the costumes during the daytime and change before you head out in the evening.

Even if you don't get costumes for the boys, one for the groom is essential, the general aim being to make him look like a complete prat. The old lady's dress idea works well, for example – and finishing it off with a nice matching handbag and hat is the pièce de résistance that will mark you out as an über godlike best man rather than just your common or garden one.

A quick search on the internet will reveal a million different stag night pranks to play on the groom, from the fairly harmless stripogram or making him a special cocktail containing far too many vodka shots to be healthy, to the classic combination of nudity, handcuffs and an immoveable object. Use your imagination and you'll definitely be able to come up with something pretty good, but also use your common sense. By all means make fun of him and embarrass him, but don't take it too far. You're in charge and you know the groom best, so you should know what he will and won't be up for.

Final thoughts before the stag night...

At least a week before the stag night send out a final email to everyone detailing the exact plan, including where you're meeting, contact details for your hotel and activity centres, and a list of any particular things they need to bring. Make sure you have everyone's mobile number, and double-check all hotel and activity bookings as well as the travel reports before you leave.

Make sure you have:

- your phone – charged and topped up if it's pay as you go
- plenty of cash
- contact details for all the stags
- all booking references and venue contact details
- any train or plane tickets and passports if needed
- some local taxi numbers
- all your props and games
- some headache pills.

The big day

Hopefully it will all go exactly to plan, the groom won't be harmed in any way, you won't lose anyone and everybody will have a jolly old time before heading home safely. Follow a few essential top tips and you won't go far wrong.

- Before the stag night call ahead to any nightclubs you plan to visit and try to get your names on the guest list. Just before you get to the club – even if your group aren't being particularly rowdy – split up into pairs and join the queue separately. Arrange to meet at the bar once you're all inside. Try not to draw attention to yourselves in the queue, as bouncers can be notoriously unfriendly to stag nights and it would be a shame for the local Door Hitler to spoil your night.

- Let all the stags know the general plan of activities so if you lose anyone they should be able to catch you up at the next venue. They're all grown men, though, so you can't be expected to be responsible for everyone all of the time. Keep an ear out for your phone just in case.

- If you lose the groom this is more of a problem, and you as the best man need to find him. Don't try to do it with all the other stags in tow. Leave them where they are and arrange to meet them at the next venue or back at the hotel. Then retrace your steps.

- Don't get so drunk that you can't remember your own name let alone where you're supposed to be next. You need to be in charge of the group so try not to get truly obliterated until most of your duties are done and dusted. Sneak in the odd glass of water when no one's looking so you can give the impression of keeping up with the rest of the group.

- Be prepared and have a few crafty drinking games up your sleeve to get the party started and liven things up if it all gets a bit subdued. Turn to page 113 for places to find good ideas.

- There is a good reason why stag parties are banned from a number of bars and clubs in city centres – so many of the men behave really, really badly. Don't let your group be one of these and you'll have a better night because of it. You can still have a right old laugh without anyone throwing a punch, being sick or ending up in a cell.

- Make sure somewhere near where you fall asleep is some water and some aspirin. Also find out the location of the nearest establishment serving big fat fried breakfasts so you can just stumble there the following morning without even opening your eyes.

And finally…

What happens on the stag night *goes no further*. Make sure all the stags know this. When asked by your inquisitive girlfriend – who will certainly call all the other stags' girlfriends the moment you divulge any information – be annoyingly vague and tell her you had a fantastic time but can't really think of any one thing particularly worth mentioning. She won't believe you, but it will hold her off. Definitely don't show her the photos – that's down to the groom if he really wants to do it!

4

The Speech

If there's one aspect of the best man's role that causes people to consider turning the job down it's the speech. And, unfortunately for you, the main things people remember about a wedding after the event are probably what the bride wore and how good the speeches were. But don't worry – help is at hand.

If you're not blessed with the gift of the gab and the last time you stood up in front of a crowd to speak was in a junior school assembly, don't panic. There are plenty of tricks of the trade used by experienced public speakers that you can also employ to make sure yours is a great speech and – even if you're nervous as hell – to make yourself look like a consummate professional.

The general order of things

Traditionally, the father of the bride speaks first. He thanks all the guests for coming and then usually says a few words about his daughter before proposing a toast to the happy couple. After he's sat down, the groom speaks. He thanks the father of the bride for his speech and his toast, speaks about how happy he is today and says something about his fantastic new wife. He also gives out thank you gifts to the wedding party and anyone else who may have helped out, which you may need to assist him with. He finishes by toasting the bridesmaids.

It's becoming more common now for the bride to say a few words too, either giving a joint speech with the groom or standing up to speak after him. Occasionally, the chief bridesmaid also makes a speech. This can be fitted into the order of speeches wherever it seems most appropriate. The best man's is always the most anticipated speech, so it's generally saved until last.

Your major responsibilities are:

- to act as toastmaster – if there isn't one – and introduce all the other speakers
- to help the groom give out any thank you presents
- to thank the groom (during your speech) on behalf of the bridesmaids for his toast and also offer vicarious thanks from any other attendants who have been toasted
- to read out any messages from absent friends and relatives
- to give a humorous speech with plenty of anecdotes about the groom, finding a tone that will appeal to both his lewdest mates and his grandma, being both inoffensive and entertaining
- to propose a toast to the happy couple.

Getting started

As soon as you're asked to be best man you should start mulling the speech over in your mind and if you have any immediate ideas jot them down. No later than three months before the wedding you need to start thinking about it in earnest and get some proper notes down on paper. You should aim to finish the basic plan about a month before the wedding so you have plenty of time to practise your speech and do a little fine-tuning.

50

The Speech

Start by sitting down with a note pad and writing down any stories about the groom that come to mind, as well as a few bullet points about his personal traits, hobbies or achievements. If some of the stories are bit inappropriate for a wedding, remember that you don't have to tell the whole story – just leave out any parts that aren't clean enough to recite in front of his grandma.

If you're short on stories, speak to his siblings for comedy childhood tales or to any of your other friends who might be able to suggest some ideas. The right sort of material could include what he was like as a child, his first car, family holidays, pets, his first job, and strange childhood habits or hobbies. If you've known the groom since you were young there should hopefully be some school or university stories worth recounting. If you haven't known him that long, think about what you've done together, maybe afternoon sessions in the pub, holidays or funny football incidents in the local park.

You could try asking his parents for a good childhood tale or two, or see if you can lay your hands on some of his old school reports for inspiration. If there are any suitable stories from the stag night – i.e. not involving strippers, nakedness or too much drunken debauchery – then you could include them. Remember, you only really need two decent ones.

Structuring your speech

1 Starting well

Starting with a cracking opening line will get the audience on your side – and getting a laugh right at the beginning will help to put you at your ease. Something along the lines of 'This speech is brought to you in association with Immodium' will raise a giggle and let the audience know that you're a wee bit nervous but they should bear with you. Never start by apologising for how bad the speech is going to be. It will lower the guests' expectations and get things off the ground on the wrong note – and if you tell them it's going to be a bad speech, it probably will be.

Other examples of good opening lines include:

- 'Typical! This is the first time (the groom) has ever bought me dinner and I was so nervous about the speech I couldn't eat it.'
- 'I'm sure you'll agree with me, gentlemen, today is a sad day for single men, as another beauty leaves the available list. And, ladies, I'm sure you'll agree that today is passing by without much of a ripple.'
- 'Well, it's said that being asked to be the best man is like being asked to make love to the Queen Mother: it's a great honour but nobody wants to do it.'

SURVIVAL TIP 10

The internet is a great source of witty one-liners that are great for a snappy intro (see pages 115–116 for links), but be wary of using more than one or two, and choose carefully from the wealth available. Many just won't be applicable to your groom at all, and if you try to compose the entire thing from one-liners gleaned from the web, it will be totally obvious and the speech will sound impersonal and formulaic. There's also a good chance that some of your audience will have heard your jokes before.

2 Thanks and congratulations

After the intro there's a whole lot of thanking to be done before you launch into the speech proper. First of all, you should thank the other speakers for their speeches. Next, thank the newlyweds on behalf of the bridesmaids, and then congratulate the wedding couple on having just got married. Finally, compliment the bride on how gorgeous she looks.

3 Stories about the groom

Next, you start talking about the groom, perhaps telling a couple of tales about when he did something very stupid or got very drunk, or talking about funny things he likes to spend his time on. These stories should be chosen carefully so that they don't embarrass him too much – mildly embarrassed rather than totally humiliated is what you're aiming for. They shouldn't be so rude that they outrage any elderly relatives or so inappropriate that they upset the bride, his new in-laws or his parents. Finally, they must be stories that everyone can share in. There's no point in telling some in-joke involving people and places that only a few of his close mates will understand or find funny.

4 Appreciation of the groom

After the embarrassing stories, you should get serious for a minute and say something heartfelt and sincere about the groom. This may go against all your manly instincts, but it doesn't have to be super-slushy. You need to say something along the lines of how he's been a good mate to you, what an all-round good guy he is and how you hope he will be very happy with his new wife. If that makes you really uncomfortable, you can always follow it up with a little joke about there being sick bags outside the room for any guests that need them.

5 Reading the messages

If there are any telegrams or messages – or these days emails – from absent friends and relatives, you should read them out at this point. If there aren't many or they're a bit dry, you could add a few funny ones of your own from obviously made-up people.

6 The toast

Finally, propose a toast to the happy couple and get all the guests to raise their glasses. Then you can finally sit back and relax, job well done, with a large glass of wine.

Ideas...

The format laid out on the previous pages is the traditional structure, but as long as you include all the important thank yous and so on, there's no reason why you shouldn't come up with something a little bit different or more imaginative.

- Give the speech together with the ushers or perhaps with the chief bridesmaid.
- There's nothing like a few good props to get the audience's attention and give you something to focus on rather than your own nerves. For instance, you could give a short slide show of pictures of the groom to accompany your anecdotes, or have a stand ready to display a funny picture of the groom, aged five.

> ## SURVIVAL TIP 11
>
> *If public speaking is just not you and you really can't tell a joke, no matter how many times you've practised it, the safest option is to keep your speech short but sincere. If this is your plan, tell the groom first – although being a good friend he should already know if cracking gags is just not your strong point.*

- Put together a spoof documentary with clips of family and friends sharing their thoughts about the couple. Include re-enactments of important moments in the couple's lives – acted out by friends in bad wigs.

- Put together a big box marked 'Marriage Survival Kit' and pull out of it random props – for example washing-up gloves, a football shirt, bandages, Viagra, a Spiderman costume – to go with your stories.

- Make up a spoof CV for the groom and read out some of his 'achievements'.

- At appropriate moments in your speech, display some things from the groom's childhood – toys, security blankets and so on – the kind of thing his mother has stashed away somewhere and may be persuaded to hand over to you.

It's best not to mention...

Certain subjects are always best avoided, such as race, religion, ex-partners, relatives who have refused to attend, any family squabbles or any last-minute wobbles about the wedding on the part of either the bride or the groom. Here are some more don'ts:

- Don't swear.
- Don't make any comment on the couple's suitability for each other, no matter what your feelings are on the matter.
- Don't bring up the fact that one of the newlyweds is a divorcee.
- Don't mention any serious bad habits such as drinking, gambling or fighting.
- Don't bring up the fact that the groom is a bit of a womaniser.
- Don't make fun of the bride.
- Don't make racist, sexist or homophobic comments – you'll only make yourself look like an idiot.
- Don't make dirty adult jokes – even if there are no children present.
- Don't make fun of the bride's parents, the bridesmaids, the wedding ceremony or the reception.

Getting the experts in

Your speech will be more personal if you write it yourself, but if you really don't feel you can do this, or if you have very little time to spare, there are plenty of experts out there who will write your speech for you (see pages 115–116 for contact details). A professional speechwriter can compose the whole thing from scratch if you give him a few details about the groom, or he can tidy up a speech you have composed yourself. There are also companies that will write a funny poem about the groom to be incorporated into your own speech.

If the problem isn't the writing but the presentation, think about having some sessions with a coach, who will be able to help you present yourself correctly and speak clearly.

Nerves – who needs them?

The best way to deal with nerves before the big day is to be completely prepared. If you've spent time working on your speech to make it as good as possible, practised it a few times and got some honest feedback from someone who knows the couple, you should have nothing to worry about.

SURVIVAL TIP 12

Be prepared for any 'amusing' friends who think it'll be a laugh to heckle you. Have a couple of witty retorts ready, such as 'I thought alcoholics were supposed to be anonymous' or 'Is your village missing its idiot?', which will hopefully shut them up and allow you to wow everyone else with your quick wit.

Top tips for overcoming nerves

- Practise, practise, practise. It's boring but practice really does make perfect, and you will feel more confident if the words just roll off your tongue.
- It may help to practise in front of a camcorder so you can look at your stance and hear how the words sound.
- Write key phrases on cue cards to remind you of the main points in case you forget. It's best to avoid reading your speech verbatim, as this may mean that you hide behind your papers and never look up. Also, if you're nervous, paper can flap around, while cue cards look steadier.
- Practise projecting your voice so that you sound confident even if you're not feeling it. Try this at home in front of your girlfriend or a mate who will give you honest feedback.
- Commit as much of your speech to memory as you can, so that you can look at the audience when you're speaking. If you can't memorise all of it, at least get the opening lines off pat, and then try to look up as much as possible while you're reading from your sheet.

On the day

Follow these guidelines before you actually speak to make sure that your delivery is as good as you can possibly make it:

- Have a quick read through of your speech somewhere quiet ten minutes before the speeches start so it's all fresh in your mind. Head to the toilet at the same time and also smarten up your hair, straighten your tie and check your teeth for spinach.

SURVIVAL TIP 13

Keep the speech in your jacket pocket but make sure you print out a spare copy, which you have in your overnight bag, just in case.

- Have a glass of water nearby in case your mouth dries up.
- Make sure you take a few deep breaths before you stand up, and focus on breathing properly throughout the speech. This will both improve your delivery and help to calm you down. Have a quick look at the audience too. They will have had a few drinks, been warmed up by the previous two speeches and be looking forward to enjoying yours. Think positive.
- As you stand up, don't sandwich yourself between your chair and the table. Push your chair in and use it to rest your weight on if need be. Stand up confidently and don't be afraid to take your time and get into a good position.
- Speak loudly and try not to rush. If you're nervous, it's tempting to speed through your speech, but if you do that, it will come across as garbled. Guests won't know what you're saying and therefore you won't get the responses you're after.
- Have a glass or two of Dutch courage but not too many. You will definitely embarrass yourself if you try to deliver your speech drunk, and it will be caught on someone's camera for all time. Just picture the clips of drunken best men from *You've Been Framed* if you feel yourself reaching for a third drink.
- If you're feeling really nervous, try just to look at the table closest to you so you don't feel overwhelmed by the number of people.

So what are you worried about?

What's actually the worst thing that can happen? You're going to get laughs because after a couple of months of planning it, your speech can't be anything but well written; and the people at the back will be able to hear you because you'll have practised speaking clearly and loudly at home in front of a friend. Remember that all the people watching will want you to do well, and probably quite a few of them will be good friends, so no one's going to throw anything or start slow handclapping. The perfect best man's speech is one that's relaxed and heartfelt. No one will expect a comedy routine worthy of Jonathan Ross, so just be yourself, tell a couple of stories and wish the couple well and you can't go far wrong.

Basically, to get the best man's speech right you simply have to make sure you follow a few golden rules:

- Be entertaining and sincere.
- Try not to get carried away. Any more than ten minutes is too long.
- One or two short anecdotes is enough – and you don't need to include all the long-winded gory details.
- By all means embarrass the groom, but only slightly.
- Don't offend anyone, particularly elderly relatives, parents and parents-in-law and, most importantly, the bride. 'If in doubt, leave it out' should be your decision-making mantra.
- Whatever happens, remember to finish with a toast to the happy couple.

5

And the Rest…

We've covered the best man's major
responsibilities, but to do the job properly there are one
or two – okay, a few – other things that you need to
think about. If you can get these bases covered, you will
make life a lot easier for the groom – and you'll be
remembered as a really brilliant best man.

Transport

Part of your job involves looking after some of the transport arrangements for the day, such as getting the groom to the ceremony on time. This generally means either that the groom hires some kind of fantastic car, which one of you drives the pair of you to the church in together, or you drive him in your own car.

If he's going for the first option, you're a lucky man – unless his idea of a fantastic car is a replica of *The Duke's of Hazzard's* General Lee or Del Boy's wheels from *Only Fools and Horses*. Don't laugh, both of these are hired out for weddings! More usually, though, the vehicle will be something that the groom has always wanted to drive, such as a cool sports car or a classic car. If he's too nervous to drive it himself, you may get the job, so before the wedding, check that you are fully insured to drive it and find out where you should pick it up and when it has to be returned.

If you're really keen on picking up the award for the best best man ever, you could consider surprising the groom with a great car to travel in on the morning of the wedding. Imagine his face when instead of your old banger there's a cool E-Type Jag waiting for him. Often it's the bride who gets all the big treats on the wedding day, but maybe the groom should get some too.

If you're using your own car, give it a bit of a pre-wedding clean. You don't have to go to town, but you may also be required to give people lifts after the ceremony, so at the very least take out the empty crisp packets and bottles of coke and give it a squirt of air freshener. More importantly, check that it's in a reliable condition – if there's any hint of smoke or a smell of burning coming from it the week before the wedding, make alternative plans.

SURVIVAL TIP 14

However reliable you think your chosen mode of transport is, make sure you have a few local taxi numbers on hand just in case. On no account plan to take public transport – you'll be laughed at by your fellow travellers, and you'll probably be late. Take a cab.

Your transport responsibilities also stretch to looking after the guests' transport between the ceremony and reception. Guests should get in touch before the wedding if they don't have transport between the two venues, but it might be worth finding out who in the wedding party – such as the ushers or the parents of both bride and groom – has a spare place in their car for anyone who needs it on the day. There's bound to be someone who doesn't plan ahead and you don't want to leave anyone stranded, or have to make extra trips yourself to ferry people around. You may even be expected to fork out for guests' taxis if no other transport can be found for them – discuss this in advance with the bride and groom to see if this is the arrangement. With a bit of forward planning, taxis shouldn't be necessary.

Organising the ushers

It's your job to co-ordinate the ushers, making sure they all have their outfits and know where they're meant to be and when. If you don't know them all, it might be a good idea to meet up before the wedding and discuss their responsibilities. You may also need to help the groom co-ordinate getting both the ushers and the fathers of the bride and groom in the same place at the same time for a suit fitting. It doesn't have to be a formal occasion. Perhaps you can get together for a drink. If you live quite a way apart, just get on the phone or send some e-mails.

SURVIVAL TIP 15

If you arrive with the groom in a hired car, don't forget to organise your own lift to the reception. He'll probably use the car to head to the reception with his new bride and won't want you tagging along!

The ushers' main responsibilities are:

- to attend a suit fitting with the groom
- to direct drivers to parking spaces at both the ceremony and reception if necessary
- to get to the reception early, hand out orders of service and direct people to their seats as they arrive
- to help herd the right guests together at the right time for the photographs after the ceremony.

Mens
Button holes

Make sure you have all the ushers' mobile numbers in case anyone is late on the day, and if any of them seems particularly useless – don't worry, there's always one – try to give him one of the less taxing jobs, such as just turning up on the right day at the right time!

Your outfit

What you wear on the day will be up to the bride and groom and will most likely depend on the style and formality (or not) of the wedding. Morning wear is the most traditional outfit, and if that's what the groom is wearing, you and the ushers will probably wear exactly the same, apart from perhaps a slightly different waistcoat or cravat. Equally, if he has gone for a contemporary lounge suit, then normally you and the ushers will have the same, with matching ties. Somewhere in between the morning suit and the lounge suit is the frock coat, which is a suit jacket cut to fall mid-thigh – often with a Nehru collar.

Suits for the wedding party are usually hired – unless the bride and groom are feeling exceptionally flush – and the cost is generally covered by the bride and groom. However, if their budget is tight, they may ask you all to wear your own suits, with matching ties.

If you are a female best man, you will need to liaise with the bride about what you wear. She should be the centre of attention at the altar, and you don't want your outfit to outshine hers in any way. Discuss the kind of thing she would prefer you to wear and in what colours so there's no chance of upsetting her.

Accessories

You may never have consciously accessorised an outfit in your entire life, but don't worry, you'll be told exactly what you need to wear. It's an unusual groom who goes for the full top hat, cane and white gloves combo, but the top hat without the other accessories is fairly popular choice. Unfortunately, after it's served its purpose during the ceremony and in the photographs you'll spend the rest of the day putting it down, forgetting where you left it and mixing it up with other people's until at the end of the night you find that it's either been used as a rubbish bin or the groom's niece has been sick in it.

SURVIVAL TIP 16

Check that you have cufflinks – these will probably be the only accessory you need to supply yourself. If you're being really organised, make sure you have a spare pair on the day, as someone else is bound to forget theirs.

To help save yourself some of this hassle, it's worth pointing out to the groom that while most hire companies offer an accidental damage waiver for the suits, top hats are often not covered by this because so many groom's men lose them. If that fails and he's still keen, you'll have to grin and bear it and just try to keep track of as many hats as you can, because it's more than likely that it will be you in the hire shop after the wedding forking out for the cost of any missing ones.

Keeping the bride happy

This is an important one. Your main job is obviously to help out the groom in any way you can, but keeping the bride on side will make both your lives a lot easier. The size of this task will depend entirely on what kind of bride you are dealing with, although even the sweetest bride can have her bridezilla moments when things aren't going her way. Just so you can recognise the tell-tale signs and protect yourself in time, the unofficial dictionary definition of bridezilla is as follows:

> **Bridezilla** *n. a woman who, in the run-up to her wedding day, has taken on some of the terrifying characteristics of Godzilla, creature of the deep, in her quest for the perfect big day. Known by the mad-eyed, unblinking stare caused by spending too many hours sticking together diamante-encrusted wedding invitations, and her crazed roaring when confronted with a delivery of the wrong colour napkin rings, her defining characteristic is a total lack of control or reason where her wedding day is concerned. Use caution when approaching.*

If this is what you are dealing with, be afraid – be very afraid – and be careful not to put a foot wrong.

If the bride has any major concerns, she will probably raise them with you in her own time, but it will earn you brownie points if you can pre-empt her. If you think she might be worried about the stag night, have a quiet word and reassure her that even though you've been winding the groom up, he won't actually come to any harm. If you think she's worried about the morning of the wedding, show her your timetable of things to do, so she knows you've got it all under control. There's a good chance she may give you a timetable of her own

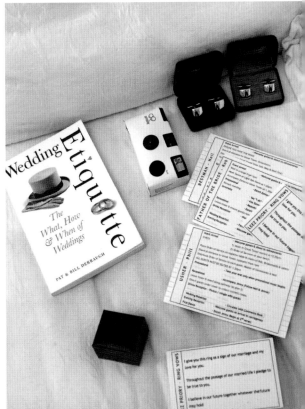

devising. This could range from a simple list of all the jobs you need to do right through to your own personalised minute-by-minute schedule of the big day, including exactly what you're supposed to be doing when. Whichever version it is, accept it with good grace and reassure her that you'll follow it to the letter – then give it your best shot!

Collecting the orders of service and buttonholes

This will be your job but could potentially be delegated to a trustworthy usher. You may be able to collect the orders of service from the printers in the week preceding the wedding, but the buttonholes will probably only be ready on the morning of the big day. Make sure you factor both of these tasks into your schedule.

The rings

The best man who forgot/lost the wedding rings is the ultimate urban myth. Now and again, though, it does actually happen – there's no smoke without fire – so don't completely rule out the possibility. You will generally be responsible for the rings from the moment you and the groom leave the house up to the point when you hand them over during the wedding ceremony. Just be sensible, check you have them before leaving the house – make sure you're still safely inside and not near a sink – and then don't check them again until ten minutes before the ceremony. Definitely don't take them out of the box until asked to by the celebrant – especially not near any open drains, street sweepers, or small hungry dogs, or in very high winds.

Looking after the honeymoon documents and luggage

A few weeks before the wedding, check with the groom that he has everything sorted for the honeymoon, particularly if this is solely his responsibility. Make sure he has everything he needs, including up-to-date passports, visas and inoculations, in case anything has slipped his mind. If the couple are going on honeymoon straight after the wedding, make sure that before leaving the house on the day you check that all the important documents are with his honeymoon luggage. Also give the house a quick once over as you leave to make sure all the windows are shut, the oven is off and so on.

If the couple aren't going away immediately, they will still need some overnight luggage, and in the organised chaos of the wedding day this can be forgotten until it's too late. It's not unusual for happy newlyweds to stumble to bed after their reception to find that their overnight bags are locked in the boot of someone else's car. Make sure you allow five minutes at some point during the reception to arrange for their luggage to be taken up to their room.

Does the groom have everything?

Finally, keep in close contact with the groom and make sure that he's coping with everything okay, as he may be feeling a bit nervous and disorganised. If you want to be a really great best man, don't sit back and wait to be asked; give him a call a few times in the last few weeks before the wedding and offer to help. It may be that all he needs is for you to go out with him for the night and take his mind off all the wedding planning, but you won't know if you don't ask.

> ### SURVIVAL TIP 17
>
> *If the groom's getting a proper shave on the morning of the wedding, see if you can join him. If you've never had one before, it's a real treat and will help to relax you both before the off – as well as giving you skin like a baby's bottom.*

Get scrubbed up

If you've been thinking about a haircut, try to get it done a few weeks before the wedding to give it time to settle in or to correct any disasters if it all goes horribly wrong. The bride and groom are probably going to be spending lots of money on lovely wedding photographs that will include you – and then have to look at them for years to come – so you owe it to them to look your best. Don't choose this moment to go for anything crazy or new – just have a trim. You don't want to scare the couple's elderly relatives with a skinhead or a Mohican that you decided just at the last minute would be a laugh.

Your present

Don't forget, you're still supposed to get the happy couple a wedding present. Unfortunately, giving up the last few months of your life to help plan their wedding isn't enough; you need to cough up some cash for that great blender or those must-have pots and pans from their gift list. Try to order something from the list at least a couple of weeks before the wedding, and if it's not being delivered by the gift list company, give it to the bride and groom the week before so you don't have to deal with it on the day.

The Final Countdown

After months of preparation, at last the wedding is imminent. If both you and the groom have survived the stag do and the wedding's still on, you can be assured that you're doing a great job so far. Now you need to stay up to speed with your tasks in the final week before the wedding.

The week before the wedding

If at all possible, try to book a couple of days off work, but if you can't manage that, at least try to get the day before the wedding off.

Collect the suits

Your first job this week will probably be to collect the suits from the hire shop or help the groom to do it. If possible, when you initially go for a fitting, make a list of all the wedding party's sizes so that when you pick up your order you can check that everything is there and in the right size. Make sure that both you and the groom try on your outfits as soon as possible so there is plenty of time to correct any mistakes. Get the rest of the wedding party to do the same. It's not unheard of for the best man to have to spend the whole of the wedding day with his jacket done up because the waistcoat delivered was too small, or even worse in a pair of trousers that are blatantly too short because he didn't check before the day.

New shoes

If you've got new shoes for the occasion, make sure you wear them around the house a bit so they don't rip your feet to shreds on the day. Also make sure the soles are a little scuffed so that as you race up the aisle to let the groom know the bride's here, you don't go flying.

Ushers' duties

Email or call the ushers this week and allocate the different duties, such as car parking, giving out orders of service and directing people to their seats, so each one knows what they are responsible for.

Travel arrangements

Check all hire car bookings and plan your route to the venue. If you're travelling any distance, check Teletext or on the internet for any planned road works. Make sure you take into account the time of day – if it's rush hour you'll need to allow a little more time.

Pack your own overnight bag

While you're busy worrying about the groom don't forget you'll need one or two things yourself to get you through the day. Apart from all the obvious overnight stuff – spare pants, a toothbrush and that sort of thing – make sure you include the following:

- an extra copy of your speech
- any props you need for the speech
- decorations for the couple's car
- booking details for your hotel room
- any paperwork such as the wedding licence and/or certificate of banns
- local taxi numbers
- details of the hire shop so you can return the suits the next day
- contact numbers for all the ushers.

Also call and confirm that your hotel booking for the wedding is still okay – and make another one if it isn't!

Give the couple their wedding present

Pretty self-explanatory this one, just get it out of the way nice and early so you can think about everything else.

The day before the wedding

This is your last day to finalise any plans. Your speech should be finished and sounding good, but give it a last read through just in case. Make sure you've also done the following important tasks:

- Charged your phone and put money on it if it's pay as you go.
- Got a wad of cash out of the bank – you will need it for bar bills, taxis and a million other unexpected things.
- Got your clothes all ready – shirt ironed, shoes polished and so on.

The rehearsal

The wedding rehearsal is usually the night before the wedding, but if this time is tricky for the bride and groom it can take place at any point during the week before the wedding. Its main purpose is to show all the main players – the couple, their parents, the best man and the chief bridesmaid – where they're supposed to be and what they're supposed to do during the ceremony. It's not usually necessary for the ushers to attend the rehearsal. If it's a religious service, the celebrant will be there guiding the proceedings. If it's a civil ceremony, the registrar isn't normally present but usually someone from the venue will tell you what you should be doing.

> ## SURVIVAL TIP 18
>
> *Don't wear your wedding outfit to the rehearsal. It's not needed and you'll look like a wally.*

Make sure you find out where you're supposed to be throughout the ceremony and at which points you're supposed to be seated or to stay standing. Ensure that you are clear on the general running order and listen carefully to the wedding vows so you know roughly when you're expected to hand over the rings.

This may also be the first time you see the venue, so take advantage of the opportunity to find out a few things that will help you later on at the wedding. Make sure you know where:

- you and the groom will stand
- the ushers will stand to give out the orders of service
- the toilets are situated – people are bound to ask you
- guests can park
- the couple want to have their photographs taken.

Try to take a moment to chat to the celebrant or venue co-ordinator so that if they have any problems on the day or if anything is going wrong they can let you know about it, and vice versa. Also make a note of the names of any flowergirls or pageboys and who their parents are. Hopefully, you won't have to be in charge of them, but if you suddenly have to deal with a tantrum in the church it's handy to know where to find mum and dad.

SURVIVAL TIP 19

This is your final chance to allay everyone's fears by turning up on time, looking respectable, and being generally helpful and considerate. It's probably too late now for the groom to find a replacement, but just in case!

The rehearsal dinner

In the US, the rehearsal dinner can be almost as lavish as the wedding breakfast, with invitations, decorations, favours and so on. Fortunately, the British are still happy with something a bit more low-key. In the UK, the rehearsal dinner is usually a nice meal to which everyone involved in the rehearsal is invited, either at a local pub or restaurant, or at the home of the parents of the bride or groom. The idea is simply to allow everyone to get to know each other so the actual day feels more relaxed and friendly.

Remember to be on your best behaviour, as you'll be with the couple's close family and you want to make a good impression. Try not to drink too much, particularly if the dinner is taking place the night before the wedding. You don't want to embarrass yourself or have a hangover the next day.

The night before

By this point you should have discussed with the groom where you are both staying the night before the big day. A lot will depend on the bride's plans. You will probably both stay at the groom's home if the bride is at her parents', or at your home if the bride will be at theirs, or in hotel rooms at or near the reception venue. Unless it's impossible – or the couple are being less than traditional and staying together – try to stay in the same place as the groom. It will make things a lot easier the following morning and reduce the risk of you getting caught in traffic, for example, and not being there on time to wake him up, check he has everything and so on.

If you have the rehearsal and accompanying dinner the night before the wedding, half your night will have been safely taken up with family and friends. If not, it may be tempting to invite all the ushers round and have a night with the boys. This isn't a good plan as it is more than likely to end with both you and the groom legless and up until the small hours talking rubbish and playing computer games. You should have done all your drinking at the stag do; this is one night when it's a really good idea to head to bed at a reasonable hour having had only one or two. For one thing, it's your job to get the groom to the wedding in good shape, but there's your own condition to consider as well. Just imagine how it will feel to have to deal with relatives, children, photographers and an angry bride, all with a hangover. If it all goes wrong after you have diligently read your way through this book and done so much work, it will be a terrible shame. The best plan is for you and the groom to spend the evening alone together, maybe with a takeaway and a video to distract him from any nerves, and then early to bed.

Make certain that you both set an alarm for the following morning, and if in any doubt also set a third one. If you can't stay with the groom, the night before the wedding call him to check he's set his alarm, then call him again first thing in the morning to check it's actually gone off. Everyone's seen that clip from the beginning of *Four Weddings and a Funeral*; don't let that mad expletive-laden dash to get to the church on time be how your groom spends the last hour of his life as a single man.

The Morning and the Ceremony

This is it, the day when all your months of careful planning will, hopefully, come to fruition! You've done your groundwork and everything is in place and ready to go. All that remains to make a success of the big day is to pay attention to the last-minute timing

First thing in the morning

As soon as your alarm goes off, go and bang on the groom's door and check that he's awake. Make him a cup of tea and then go back and make certain he's awake. Whatever time of day the wedding is, you'll be probably have to be up at a decent hour to make sure that everything that needs to get done is done.

If it's an early wedding, there may be no time to do anything other than shower, get dressed and then head out. If the wedding isn't until the afternoon, you may have a couple of hours to kill.

Since most grooms won't take quite as long as their bride to get ready, you might want to think of something nice to do during the morning that will help to take the groom's mind off the impending nuptials. For example you could:

- book in for an early round of golf
- hire a couple of films
- go to a professional barbers and get a wet shave
- send the groom out for a morning run or a swim if this is something he usually enjoys, so he can calm his nerves while you make him a good breakfast.

SURVIVAL TIP 19

Make sure you both eat a hearty breakfast. This is most important for the groom, but you also need to eat a decent meal. You may not eat again until the wedding breakfast, which will be a good few hours away, and a couple of glasses of champagne on an empty stomach is not a good idea when you need to keep a clear head.

Your 'to do' list for the wedding morning

Make sure that you have all the following covered:

- Eat breakfast.

- Get into your outfit (after breakfast in case of spillages!)

- Take any labels off the soles of your shoes.

- Call all the ushers and check that everything's running to plan.

- Collect the buttonholes and orders of service.

- Check out your transport – i.e. call the cab company to confirm your booking, pick up the hire car or start your own car just in case.

- Remind the groom to call his fiancée and to send his present round to her if he's sending one.

- Check where the rings are.

- Check the traffic reports for any delays on your route.

- Make sure the groom has his front door keys. They often get left behind in the rush to leave and the newlyweds get back to find they're locked out.

Keep calm

No matter how much of a fluster you are in, the groom is bound to be in a worse state. Try to act cool and keep him calm at the same time. Remember to tell him how great he looks in his suit.

Final checklist before leaving the house

Before you leave for the wedding make sure that you have all the following:

- overnight luggage for you and the groom
- directions
- important documents such as the wedding licence or certificate of banns
- a copy of your speech, plus a spare
- any props you need for the speech
- the buttonholes and orders of service
- your phone
- money for the celebrant and band
- decorations for the couple's car
- contact numbers for all the ushers
- the rings
- the groom!

Two hours before

Aim to be at the wedding venue two hours early to allow plenty of time for heavy traffic and unexpected delays. This will also mean you have time for a swift nerve-calming beer with the ushers before the ceremony. The groom's last beer as a free man is quite a feature of the traditional British wedding, but do make sure it's only one. The groom should be – indeed, legally must be – in a fit state to tie the knot.

At this point remind the ushers about their different duties. One or two of them should have been allocated to directing the car parking at the venue, while the rest will be handing out the orders of service inside and showing people where to sit. The buttonholes also need to be given out to the men in the wedding party and the mothers of the bride and groom, as well as sometimes the grandparents.

> *SURVIVAL TIP 20*
>
> *Ask the ushers who are directing the car parking to make sure your car isn't boxed in, as you'll need to make a speedy getaway to the reception.*

One hour before

Get to the venue for the ceremony with the ushers so you're ready to greet guests as they start to arrive. From here on in, your role at the ceremony is pretty easy. As the guests start to file in, check that the ushers are doing their job and try to keep the groom calm. Chat to him about something light-hearted to keep his mind off the impending nuptials. Ten minutes before the ceremony is due to start, check you have the rings safely in your pocket.

Seating the guests

You are not expected to seat the guests personally, as your main job is to look after the groom, but you need to make sure the seating is being done properly. This is the job of the ushers. The groom's family usually sit on the right and the bride's on the left, so make sure the ushers know this. Remind them to keep the front seats free for the bride's immediate family, particularly her parents, who will arrive last, and the bridesmaids. If the seating starts to look a little imbalanced, the ushers should seat anyone who is friends with both the bride and groom on the emptier side. Elderly relatives should be seated nearer to the front. At very formal weddings the ushers are sometimes expected to escort guests to their seats, but this can take some time and cause guests to be left waiting at the entrance.

Five minutes before

You and the groom take your places standing at the front of the venue, with you on the groom's right-hand side. One of the ushers should give you a nod so that you both know as soon as the bride has arrived.

SURVIVAL TIP 21

Don't stand up at the front too early, otherwise you'll both end up with sore feet. The bride is quite likely to be a little late, so five minutes before the ceremony is due to start is plenty of time.

Missing groom

Last-minute nerves are not totally unheard of. In the – hopefully unlikely – scenario that the groom gets cold feet at the last minute, it's your job to find him, and quickly. Gather all the ushers together and then send them out to all the most likely places he could be – the pub, the train station or hiding under his duvet. Make up some excuse and don't let anyone else know what's going on. If you find him, you may be able to talk him round, but bear in mind that he may have serious misgivings. If he can't be persuaded, it's your job to let the bride and her family know, and, unfortunately, there are likely to be a lot of tears, anger and possibly punches that, in absence of the groom, may be directed at you. It's understandable, but don't tell the bride's family where the groom is and make your exit ASAP.

The ceremony

Hopefully, though, the groom will stay exactly where he's supposed to be, and eventually the bride will make her entrance. Once she has walked up the aisle and taken her place next to the groom, the celebrant will welcome everyone and proceed with the service. Apart from the point where he asks you to hand over the rings, there's not much for you to do except look attentive and smart. If you paid attention during the rehearsal, you will probably remember when you're expected to remain standing, but if not, the celebrant will prompt you.

After the couple have exchanged their vows and given the rings, there will be a musical interlude while they sign the register. Then, as the happy couple leave the church, you should take the chief bridesmaid's arm and escort her out behind them. Immediately after the ceremony, it's usual to have the photographs.

At some point, either just before or just after the ceremony, you may need to pay the celebrant, as the groom will have other things on his mind than paying bills. He will usually have given you a cheque or cash beforehand to cover the cost.

Wedding photographs

You've probably been to a wedding where the photographs drag on and on as every possible combination of friends and family is explored. You can be instrumental in helping to get through them smoothly and quickly. The pictures may all be taken at the ceremony venue or some may be taken at the ceremony venue and others at the reception venue. Whichever is the case, organise the ushers so that while one photo is being taken they are busy finding the people who are due to be in the next one and getting them ready to step up.

The photographer is unlikely to know who all the different family members are and it's up to you to help him. Even if you don't know who everyone is yourself, you should have a good idea of which relatives will be able to point out Great Aunt Edna or Cousin Johnny. It's in your own best interests to get this part done quickly, because by this point you and all the other guests will be itching to get to the reception for a nice glass of champagne.

The Reception

Well done, you're on the home straight.

You have quite a few responsibilities at the reception – not to mention your speech – but that shouldn't mean you can't let your hair down a bit too.

Following the ceremony, and after the bride and groom have departed, ask one usher to stay behind and check there are no stragglers hanging around needing a lift while you get to the reception sharpish – the glass of chilled champagne that will no doubt be waiting for you should make that a fairly enticing task.

The drinks reception

While the bride and groom are socialising and mingling, you need to be available to deal with any problems that may arise, without worrying the newlyweds with them unless absolutely necessary. If the string quartet don't

know where to set up, for example, or the caterers aren't sure where the cake should be, you need to sort it out. You also need to be available for the other guests, who will probably want information about where they're supposed to be, what time everyone's sitting down for dinner, where the toilets are and that sort of thing. Pointing Auntie Ethel towards the loos may not be the most glamorous job in the world, but the bride and groom will appreciate you helping out so that they are free to have a good time.

SURVIVAL TIP 22

Keep track of what you're drinking. It's easy to drink more than you planned if waiters are topping up your glass while you're chatting. Remember you still need to be sober for some time to come.

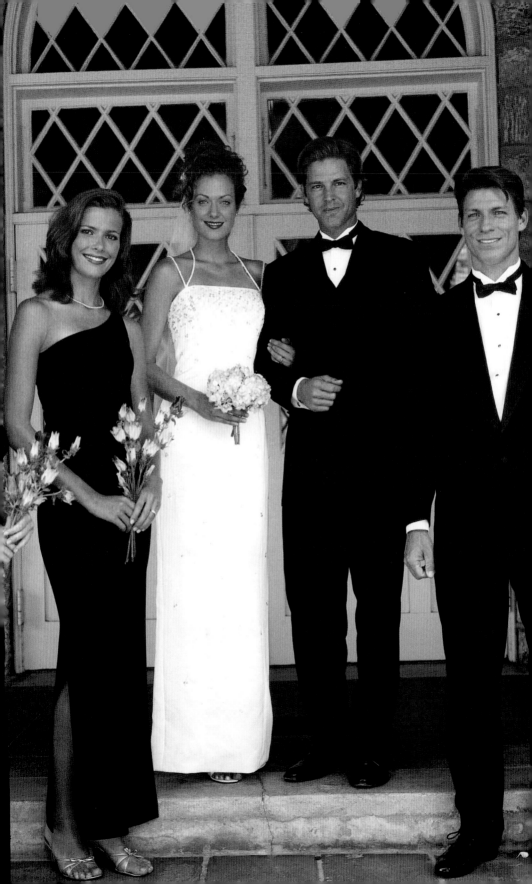

Imagine you're a fantastic host and this is your own party. You want to get it going with a swing and make sure everyone has a great time. If you see any guests looking a bit lost and lonely, make a point of socialising and checking how they are. If anyone's had a bit too much champagne already, have a quiet word with the waiters about not topping up their glass.

The receiving line

After the drinks reception comes the wedding breakfast – breakfast because it's the couple's first meal together as man and wife rather than because you're about to tuck into a full fry-up. Before the wedding, make sure you know what time everyone is due to sit down for the meal, as you're bound to be asked a hundred times by hungry guests. The venue co-ordinator will generally give the bridal party the nod about ten minutes before guests need to start filing

in so they can form the receiving line.

Traditionally, the receiving line includes the bride's and groom's parents, the bride and groom, the best man and the chief bridesmaid, in that order. The general point is that all the guests can meet all the main players in the wedding party, thank the parents and congratulate the happy couple. Unfortunately, this means that you will each have to shake hands with 100 or so people. Lovely as they'll certainly all be, even if you spend just 30 seconds saying hello to each person, it will take you over an hour to get through the lot. And you'll probably repeat something along the lines of, 'Thank you, yes, it's been lovely and, yes, I am feeling nervous about the speech' to most of them along the way!

Some couples, mindful of how long a receiving line can take, opt to save time by not including the best man and the chief bridesmaid, so keep your fingers crossed and this may be what happens in your case.

The top table

As best man, you usually get a seat on the top table, along with the happy couple, their parents and the bridesmaids. The ushers don't generally sit at the top table. Again, as with many wedding traditions, this set-up is no longer compulsory. If the newlyweds have divorced parents who don't get on or a number of step-parents, a top table is sometimes not the best idea. If one or both sets of parents are divorced it's often more practical for each parent to host their own table. Sometimes the bride and groom will choose to have a table to themselves or they may decide to share a table with you and your partner and the chief bridesmaid and hers.

Your big moment

Traditionally, the speeches follow the meal, during coffee, but it's becoming more acceptable for couples to choose to have them at the beginning of the meal if they want to. If any of the speakers is particularly nervous, having them before the meal means that everyone can then relax and enjoy their food. On the downside this means that your audience will be less well lubricated and so may be slightly less receptive than if they were full of food and wine. On the plus side, though, it means that the speakers will be less well lubricated too, and so stand a much better chance of getting through the whole thing without falling over!

Toastmaster

At this point in the proceedings, you may be starting to work yourself up into a frenzy about your speech, but before you can get on to that you may also have to act as toastmaster for the other speakers if the couple haven't hired a professional. Basically this entails getting everyone's attention and then introducing each speaker. You may also need to announce that dinner is served to get everyone to sit down at the table.

After the speech

The reception for you can probably be divided simply into two parts: pre-speech and post-speech. Once the speech is done with (turn to Chapter 4 for how get it done right) and, hopefully, no one's thrown anything at you or stormed out, you can take a deep breath and…relax. A little at least.

Depending on the time of the day when the ceremony took place, the speeches are generally followed by a slight lull as people finish their coffee, the tables are cleared away and the evening guests slowly start to arrive. Take this chance to have a breather and grab a beer, or if you're staying at the venue to nip back to your room and freshen up if need be.

The car

This is probably also a good time to sneak away and put confetti in the couple's bed – if that's the plan – and decorate their car. Things along the lines of cans/boots tied to the back bumper, shaving cream on the windscreen and filling the car full of balloons are appropriate – although not always appreciated by the happy couple. If you're feeling particularly inventive, the 'kipper on the radiator' trick is a clever one that most likely won't be discovered for a couple of days. NB: If the couple aren't leaving until the following morning, get up early the next day to do this, otherwise your beautiful shaving foam heart will have dripped onto the floor before they see it.

> ### SURVIVAL TIP 23
>
> *Make sure you don't do anything to the happy couple's car that could cause it to break down. If it stops while they're en route to the airport for their honeymoon you'll be in BIG trouble.*

First dance

Once the evening party has started in earnest, your next job will be to get all the guests together for the couple's first dance. The groom should have let you know roughly when they plan to do it and hopefully someone from the venue or the DJ will give you a nod when it's time. You'll need to let all the guests know and then with

the ushers, shepherd them over to the dancefloor with their cameras at the ready. At the end of the first dance you're expected to take to the floor with the chief bridesmaid for the next number, along with other members of the wedding party. Discuss with the bride and groom beforehand when they want you two to come in. Some couples may love their moment in the limelight and want to have it all to themselves; less confident dancers may ask you and the bridesmaid to start dancing after a minute or two because they'd rather not be up there on their own for too long.

The end of the night

After the first dance there's not much left for you to do except enjoy yourself and socialise. A really good best man will make the effort to mingle a little and act the host, ensuring everyone is having a good time. At this stage in the evening you can afford to relax and have a few drinks, but remember that you're still on show. This isn't a night out with the lads and if you get unpleasantly drunk there's still plenty of opportunity to really embarrass yourself and upset people. Try to rein it in a little.

Most wedding venues will have a fixed time when the reception has to finish. At this point you may need to help other guests find their way home, booking taxis and encouraging any remaining guests to be on their way. There may also be a certain amount of tidying up to do, collecting up flower displays and wedding presents and taking down decorations, as well as possibly settling any outstanding bar bills for the groom and paying the band. If disposable cameras were on offer at each table, make sure they are collected up.

Afterwards

Congratulations! You've completed your task as best man. Hopefully you did a good enough job for the groom to be proud of you, the bride not to hate you and the guests still to be talking about your speech a few months later.

All that remains to be done now is a little bit of tidying up for the happy couple. You've done brilliantly so far, so this is the easy bit!

Returning the suits

It usually falls to the best man to return any hire suits, and hire companies usually ask for everything back the first working day after the wedding. It's best for one person to take charge of this and return all the suits in one go rather than getting each person to return their own. If there are any stains or tears in the suits, don't be tempted to try to fix them. Normally a damage waiver fee will have been paid, so unless they're in a really terrible condition you shouldn't be charged.

Returning other hired bits and pieces

If the couple have hired crockery or table settings, you may need to return them too. There may also be vases to take back to the florist.

Table cameras

If disposable cameras were on offer at the reception, it might be nice for you to send them off to be developed so that the happy couple can pick them up after their honeymoon – check with the groom before the wedding. Don't collect the photos yourself – or if you do don't look at them – because the bride and groom should really get to see them first.

Wedding presents

If you collected up any presents or gifts of money, you may need to look after them until the bride and groom are back from their honeymoon. Make sure you store them somewhere safe and away from prying eyes. If you were handed any cash for the couple, try to get that to them before they leave if possible – they may want it for their honeymoon and you probably don't want the responsibility of it.

While they're away

If you're looking after the bride and groom's house while they are away or have access to the keys, a nice extra touch is to pop in and restock their fridge with essentials such as bread and milk, perhaps along with something nice for their first meal as a surprise. Finally, find out if the newlyweds have someone meeting them at the airport after they return from honeymoon. It's miserable having to get a train or spend money on a cab after a long journey, and meeting them at the airport will be the final job that will mark you out as the perfect best man.

Once that's accomplished you can pat yourself on the back, satisfied at a job well done. Hopefully the crazed bridezilla of previous months has morphed back into your best mate's lovely new wife and your best mate has stopped talking about flowers and sugared almonds and got back to the time-honoured bloke topics of beer and football, while you've come through the whole thing unscathed, relieved that it's all over but actually – between you and me – quietly surprised at how great a time you've had in the process.

10

Your Countdown to the Big Day

This is your cut-out-and-keep guide
to exactly what you should be doing and when.

As soon as possible / 12 months to go

☐ You find out you are best man – note the wedding date in your diary and make sure you keep the evenings of the week before clear.

9 months to go

☐ Engagement party.
☐ Help the groom choose his ushers.

6 months to go

☐ Start thinking about the stag party/weekend.
Discuss with the groom his idea of a good stag night, and then privately decide on some suitable surprises to add to this plan – but make sure they are still in keeping with the mood of the night and the feelings of the groom.
☐ Let the groom's friends know the date for the stag weekend.

4 months to go

☐ Discuss wedding plans with the bride and groom so you know who the other members of the wedding party are.
☐ Investigate transport arrangements and get something booked.
☐ Go with the groom to choose wedding outfits.

3 months to go

☐ Start writing your speech.

2 months to go

☐ Start practising your speech regularly and get feedback from someone you trust.
☐ Confirm all the stag weekend arrangements.

4 weeks to go

☐ The stag party/weekend.

☐ Buy a gift and a card for the wedding couple.

3 weeks to go

☐ Prepare a duty list for the ushers and call them to confirm what they are doing, what time they need to arrive, etc.

☐ Visit the wedding reception venue with the couple to familiarise yourself.

☐ Confirm the order of the speeches with the bride and groom.

☐ Check that the groom has the wedding rings somewhere safe.

2 weeks to go

☐ Finalise speech.

1 week to go

- ☐ Attend rehearsal dinner.
- ☐ Collect order of ceremony sheets.
- ☐ Go with the groom to collect hired outfits.
- ☐ Confirm arrangements for collecting buttonholes from the bride.
- ☐ Check with groom that all honeymoon dates have been confirmed.
- ☐ Get together decorations for couple's getaway car.
- ☐ Give the bride and groom their gift and card from you.

1 day to go

- ☐ Charge up your mobile phone.
- ☐ Withdraw plenty of cash.
- ☐ Collect letters, cards and emails from absent friends from the bride's and groom's families.
- ☐ Check that the groom has the ring and knows where it is – and that it is somewhere safe.
- ☐ Set your alarm for the following morning.

The big day

- [ ] Wake up the groom. If you're not staying with him, phone him.
- [ ] Ten minutes later, call him/knock on his door again to check he hasn't gone back to sleep.
- [ ] Phone the chief usher to check everything is under control.
- [ ] Double-check travel arrangements.
- [ ] Check clothing, accessories, money and paperwork (licence and/or certificate of banns).
- [ ] Remember the rings.
- [ ] Collect buttonholes.
- [ ] Meet at the wedding venue two hours before the wedding.
- [ ] Proceed to the nearest pub for pre-nuptial Dutch courage.
- [ ] Arrive back at the venue one hour before the ceremony.
- [ ] Check you have the rings.
- [ ] Five minutes to go, take your positions at the front of the church.

The rest of the day

After the ceremony there's no let up for the best man.

- ☐ Accompany the bridesmaids out of the church. Walk slowly and calmly.
- ☐ Outside, if confetti is allowed have a spare pack in your pocket to distribute and also to help the photographer with his 'confetti shot'.
- ☐ Help organise family and guests for the official photographs.
- ☐ Later, help direct the guests to the reception and, once there, to the receiving line (or if there isn't one then to the bar).
- ☐ Your big moment, the speech, is next on the list. Speak calmly and slowly and hopefully those weeks of practice won't let you down.
- ☐ Act the party host – encourage people onto the dance floor and try to ensure everyone is having a good time, including you.
- ☐ If they are leaving that same evening, make sure the married couple get away smoothly. Help get their bags in the car, take charge of any hire outfits to be returned and promise to look after any leftover wedding presents.
- ☐ Decorate the car – tin cans, shaving foam, you know the score – before waving goodbye.
- ☐ Pour yourself a well-earned drink.
- ☐ Finally, before you call it a day, be sure to offer your assistance to the bride's and groom's parents if there's any clearing up to do.
- ☐ And…relax. Job done.

Useful Contacts

For information on anything you don't unde
about the world of weddings, including speeches, me
and general etiquette, as well as for a – sometimes frig
– glimpse into the mind of the bride log on to
www.youandyourwedding.co.uk

Accommodation

Budget Accommodation

www.budgetaccommodation.co.uk

Best Western

www.bestwestern.co.uk

Premier Travel Inn

www.premiertravelinn.com

Travelodge

www.travelodge.co.uk

Ideas for gags, games and costumes

Bachelor Party Fun

www.bachelorpartyfun.com

Celebrations

www.celebrations-party.co.uk

Partybox

www.partybox.co.uk

Piggi Clothing

www.piggi-clothing.co.uk

Silly Jokes

www.sillyjokes.co.uk

Stag Night Out

www.stagnightout.com

The Best Man

www.thebestman.com

Grooms Online

www.groomsonline.com

Men's spa treatments

Dandy Brown's, Leeds

www.dandybrowns.com

Dress2kill Grooming, London

www.dress2killgrooming.com

E'Spa Spas, Nationwide

www.espainternational.co.uk

Gentlemen's Tonic, London

020 7297 4343

www.gentlemenstonic.com

Geo F Trumpers, London

www.trumpers.com

Jason Shankey Male Grooming,
Belfast and London

www.jasonshankey.com

Nikel London

www.nickelspalondon.co.uk

Pankhurst at Alfred Dunhill, London

020 7290 8636

Spa.NK, London

www.spacenk.co.uk

The Refinery, London

www.the-refinery.com

Menswear – to hire and buy

Austin Reed, Nationwide
0800 585479
www.austinreed.co.uk

Brooks Brothers, London
020 7256 5195

Burton Menswear, Nationwide
0800 731 8283
www.burtonmenswear.co.uk

Charles Tyrwhitt, Nationwide
www.ctshirts.co.uk

Debenhams, Nationwide
020 7408 4444
www.debenhams.co.uk

Daks, Nationwide
020 7409 4000
www.daks.com

Ede & Ravenscroft
www.edeandravenscroft.co.uk

Eton Shirts, Nationwide
www.etonshirts.co.uk

Favourbrook, Nationwide
020 7491 2337
www.favourbrook.com

Gieves & Hawkes, Nationwide
www.gievesandhawkes.com

Hackett, Nationwide
www.hackett.com

Hire Society, Nationwide
0870 780 2003
www.hire-society.com

House of Fraser, Nationwide
0870 160 7270

John Lewis, Nationwide
www.johnlewis.com

Marc Wallace, London
020 7731 4575
www.marcwallace.com

Massimo Dutti, Nationwide
www.massimodutti.com

Moss Bros Hire, Nationwide
020 7447 7200
www.mossbroshire.co.uk

Ozwald Boateng, Nationwide
www.ozwaldboateng.co.uk

Pal Zileri
020 7493 9711

Paul Smith, Nationwide
020 7836 7828
www.paulsmith.co.uk

Pierre Cardin, Nationwide
01582 509860

Pronuptia, Nationwide
01273 323046
www.pronuptia.co.uk

Ted Baker, Nationwide
www.tedbaker.co.uk

Thomas Pink, Nationwide
020 7498 3882
www.thomaspink.co.uk

Timothy Everest, London
020 7629 6236

TM Lewin, Nationwide
www.tmlewin.co.uk

Turnbull & Asser, London
www.turnbullandasser.co.uk

Young Bride & Groom, Nationwide
www.youngbrideandgroom.co.uk

Young's Hire at Suits You and Suit Direct, Nationwide
020 8327 3005
www.youngs-hire.co.uk

Pub crawls

A Beer in the Evening
www.beerintheevening.com

Pub Utopia
www.pubutopia.com

Speech quotes and jokes

AhaJokes.com
www.ahajokes.com

Hitched
www.hitched.co.uk

Love Poems and Quotes
www.lovepoemsandquotes.com

Poems For Free
www.poemsforfree.com

Wedding Speech Builder
www.weddingspeechbuilder.com

Speech writers/coaches

Advanced Public Speaking Institute
www.public-speaking.org

Alan Woodhouse, Voice Coach
www.woodhouse-voice.co.uk

Instant Speaking Success
www.instantspeakingsuccess.com

Lawrence Bernstein, Speech Writer
07970 046230
www.greatspeechwriting.co.uk

Louise Kerr, Resonance Voice Training
020 8509 2767
www.resonancevoice.com

MJ Consulting Speech Making Courses, Edinburgh
0131 466 6051
www.mjohnstonconsulting.co.uk

Presentation Helper
www.presentationhelper.co.uk/
wedding_speech

Professional Speakers Association
www.professionalspeakers.org

Skillstudio
08456 444150
www.skillstudio.co.uk

Sparkling Wedding Speeches
0800 040 7844
www.sparklingspeeches.co.uk

Speak First
www.speakfirst.co.uk

Utter Wit
www.utterwit.co.uk

Wedding Speech Builder
www.weddingspeechbuilder.com

Wordsmith etc.
0115 949 1859
davewrite2002@yahoo.com
Write 4 Me
www.write4me.co.uk

Stag nights

Atlantic Web
020 7352 1054
www.atlantic-web.com
Big Weekends
www.bigweekends.com
Blokes Only
www.blokesonly.com
Buy a Gift
www.buyagift.co.uk
Chilli Sauce
www.chillisauce.co.uk
Crocodile Events
08700 119996
www.crocodileevents.co.uk
Extreme Activities
www.extreme-activities.com
Go Ape
www.goape.co.uk
Great Experience Days
www.greatexperiencedays.co.uk
Knights Of Middle England
www.knightsofmiddleengland.co.uk
Last Night of Freedom
www.lastnightoffreedom.co.uk
Maximise
www.maximise.co.uk
Party Bus
0845 838 5400
www.partybus.co.uk

The National Karting Association
www.nationalkarting.co.uk
Red Letter Days
www.redletterdays.co.uk
Red Seven Leisure
www.redsevenleisure.co.uk
Stag Web
www.stagweb.co.uk
Stag Weekends
www.stagweekends.com
The Stag and Hen Company
www.thestagandhencompany.co.uk
The Stag Company
www.thestagcompany.com
Track Days
www.trackdays.co.uk

Transport companies

Historic & Classic Car Hirers Guild
www.hchg.co.uk
AK Vintage
www.akvintage.co.uk
American Dreams
www.americandreams.co.uk
The Antique Auto Agency
www.antique-auto-agency.co.uk
Blue Triangle Buses
www.bluetrianglebuses.com

Cabair Helicopters

www.cabairhelicopters.com

Cops and Cabbies

www.copsandcabbies.com

Courtyard Carriages

www.courtyardcarriages.co.uk

Elite Helicopters

www.elitehelicopters.co.uk

Flights 4 All

www.flights4all.com

East Midlands Helicopters

www.helicopter-services.co.uk

Karma Kabs

www.karmakabs.com

Lord Cars

www.lordcars.co.uk

Memory Lane

www.memorylane.co.uk

Star Car Hire

www.starcarhire.co.uk

Starlite Limos

www.starlitelimos.co.uk

The Marriage Carriage Company

www.themarriagecarriage
company.co.uk

The Open Road

www.theopenroad.co.uk

Wedding Carriage Company

www.wedding-carriage.co.uk

Travel links

National Rail

www.nationalrail.co.uk

The AA

www.theaa.com

National Express

www.nationalexpress.com

Cheap Flights

www.cheapflights.co.uk

Easy Jet

www.easyjet.com

Ryan Air

www.ryanair.com

Useful Contacts

Photograph Acknowledgements

Prelims: page 5 Lovegrove Photography (www.lovegroveweddings.com)

Introduction: page 7 Pal Zileri (www.palzileri.com); page 8 Moss Bros (www.mossbros.co.uk)

Chapter 1: page 10 Lovegrove Photography (www.lovegroveweddings.com); page 11 Moss Bros (www.mossbros.co.uk); page 13: Lovegrove Photography (www.lovegroveweddings.com); page 14 Pal Zileri (www.palzileri.com); pages 15, 16 and 17 Lovegrove Photography (www.lovegrove weddings.com); page 18 Guy Timewell (www.guytimewell.co.uk); page 19 Debbie Wilkinson (www.debbiewilkinson.co.uk)

Chapter 2: page 20 Pal Zileri (www.palzileri.com); pages 21 and 22 Lovegrove Photography (www.lovegroveweddings.com); page 23 Tessa Hallman/Good Housekeeping UK

Chapter 3: pages 24, 25 and 27 Lovegrove Photography (www.lovegroveweddings.com); page 28 Prima UK; pages 30, 31 and 33 Lovegrove Photography (www.lovegroveweddings.com); page 34 Sam Morgan Moore/Kitesurfing at Watergate Bay & Fototheme/Cosmo Girl UK; page 35 Buy A Gift (www.buyagift.co.uk); page 37 Lovegrove Photography (www.lovegroveweddings.com); page 38 Red Letter Days (www.redletterdays.co.uk); pages 40 and 41 Lovegrove Photography (www.lovegroveweddings.com); page 43 Timothy Everest (www.timothyeverest.com); page 44 Knights of Middle England (www.knightsofmiddleengland.co.uk); page 45 Clive Bozzard-Hill / House Beautiful UK; page 46 Cosmopolitan UK; page 47 Buy A Gift (www.buyagift.co.uk)

Chapter 4: pages 48 and 49 Lovegrove Photography (www.lovegroveweddings.com); page 50 Pal Zileri (www.palzileri.com); page 51 Marc Wallace www.marcwallace.com); page 51 Lovegrove Photography (www.lovegroveweddings.com); page 50 Pal Zileri (www.palzileri.com); page 53 Garda Tang/Hackett (www.hackett.com); page 54 Lovegrove Photography (www.lovegrove weddings.com); page 55 Pal Zileri (www.palzileri.com); page 56 Jeremy Hudson; pages 57, 58 and 59 Lovegrove Photography (www.lovegroveweddings.com); page 60 Moss Bros (www.mossbros.co.uk); page 61 Lovegrove Photography (www.lovegroveweddings.com)

Chapter 5: page 62: Marc Wallace (www.marcwallace.com); page 63 Star Car hire (www.starcarhire.co.uk); page 64 Star Car hire (www.starcarhire.co.uk); page 65 Lovegrove Photography (www.lovegroveweddings.com); page 66 Lovegrove Photography (www.lovegrove weddings.com) and Marc Wallace (www.marcwallace.com); page 67 Moss Bros (www.mossbros.co.uk); page 68 Ede & Ravenscroft (www.edeandravenscroft.co.uk); page 69 Lovegrove Photography (www.lovegroveweddings.com); page 70 Moss Bros (www.mossbros.co.uk); page 71 Lovegrove Photography (www.lovegroveweddings.com) and Studio 21/ Zest UK; page 72. Pankhurst Barbers London (www.pankhurstbarbers.com); page 73 Marc Wallace (www.marcwallace.com)

Chapter 6: page 74 Austin Reed (www.austinreed.co.uk); page 75 Phil Evans (www.philevansphoto.co.uk); page 76 House of Fraser (www.houseoffraser.co.uk); page 77 Pal Zileri (www.palzileri.com); page 78 Ede & Ravenscroft (www.edeandravenscroft.co.uk); page 79 David Clerihew / She UK; page 81 Moss Bros (www.mossbros.co.uk)

Chapter 7: page 82 Lovegrove Photography (www.lovegroveweddings.com); page 83 Garda Tang/Hackett (www.hackett.com); page 84 Ede & Ravenscroft (www.edeandravenscroft.co.uk); page 85 Oliver Sweeney (www.oliversweeney.com); page 86 Marc Wallace (www.marc wallace.com)

Chapter 8: page 90 Memory Lane (www.memorylane.co.uk); page 91 Lovegrove Photography (www.lovegroveweddings.com); page 93 Favourbrook (www.favourbrook.com); page 94 Lovegrove Photography (www.lovegroveweddings.com); page 95 Pal Zileri (www.palzileri.com); page 96 Lovegrove Photography (www.lovegroveweddings.com); page 97 Pal Zileri (www.palzileri.com); pages 98 and 99 Moss Bros (www.mossbros.co.uk)

Chapter 9: pages 100 and 101 Lovegrove Photography (www.lovegroveweddings.com); page 102 Marc Wallace (www.marcwallace.com)

Chapter 10: page 104 Pal Zileri (www.palzileri.com); page 105 Buy A Gift (www.buya gift.co.uk); page 106 Lovegrove Photography (www.lovegroveweddings.com); page 108 Garda Tang/Hackett (www.hackett.com); page 110 Debbie Wilkinson (www.debbiewilkinson.co.uk); page 111 Lovegrove Photography (www.lovegroveweddings.com); page 112 Moss Bros (www.mossbros.co.uk); page 133 Tim Imrie / House Beautiful UK; page 115 Moss Bros (www.mossbros.co.uk); page 117 Red Snapper Photography (www.red-snapper.co.uk)

For Your Notes

The wedding party

Groom's mobile . . . .

Bride's mobile . . . .

Bride's parents names and telephone . . . .

Groom's parents names and telephones . . . .

Usher's name and mobile . . . .

Usher's name and mobile . . . .

Usher's name and mobile . . . .

Usher's name and mobile . . . .

Chief bridesmaid's name and mobile . . . .

Bridesmaid's name and mobile . . . .

Bridesmaid's name and mobile . . . .

Bridesmaid's name and mobile . . . .

Bridesmaid's name and mobile . . . .

Information

Ceremony date ....

Ceremony time ....

Minister or registrar's name ....

Venue ....

Telephone ....

Reception venue ....

Contact name ....

Telephone ....

Rehearsal date and time ....

Stag night notes

Date and time ....

Meeting point ....

Guests ....

....

....

....

....

....

....

....

....

....

....

....

....

Speech notes

For Your Notes

Speech notes

Outfit notes

Budget notes

Transport notes

Index

Index